D1558012

GREAT LIGHTHOUSES OF NORTH AMERICA™

NAVESINK TWIN LIGHTS

The First U.S. Lighthouse to Use a Fresnel Lens

AILEEN WEINTRAUB

The Rosen Publishing Group's
PowerKids Press™
New York

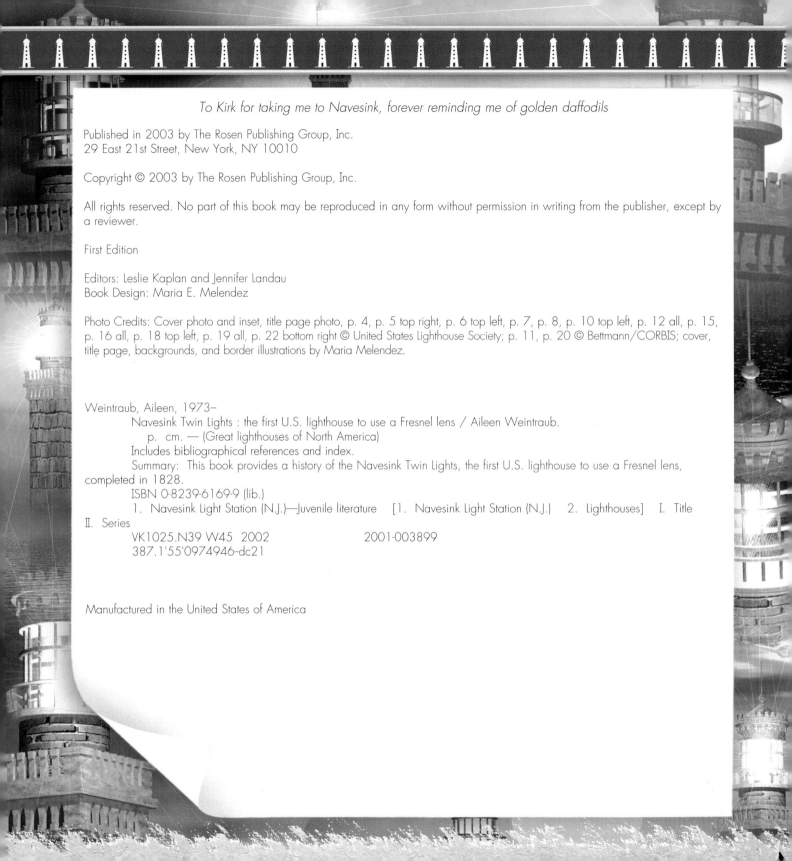

To Kirk for taking me to Navesink, forever reminding me of golden daffodils

Published in 2003 by The Rosen Publishing Group, Inc.
29 East 21st Street, New York, NY 10010

First Edition

Editors: Leslie Kaplan and Jennifer Landau
Book Design: Maria E. Melendez

Photo Credits: Cover photo and inset, title page photo, p. 4, p. 5 top right, p. 6 top left, p. 7, p. 8, p. 10 top left, p. 12 all, p. 15, p. 16 all, p. 18 top left, p. 19 all, p. 22 bottom right © United States Lighthouse Society; p. 11, p. 20 © Bettmann/CORBIS; cover, title page, backgrounds, and border illustrations by Maria Melendez.

Weintraub, Aileen, 1973–
        Navesink Twin Lights : the first U.S. lighthouse to use a Fresnel lens / Aileen Weintraub.
            p. cm. — (Great lighthouses of North America)
        Includes bibliographical references and index.
        Summary: This book provides a history of the Navesink Twin Lights, the first U.S. lighthouse to use a Fresnel lens, completed in 1828.
        ISBN 0-8239-6169-9 (lib.)
        1. Navesink Light Station (N.J.)—Juvenile literature   [1. Navesink Light Station (N.J.)   2. Lighthouses]   I. Title
II. Series
        VK1025.N39 W45 2002   2001-003899
        387.1'55'0974946–dc21

Manufactured in the United States of America

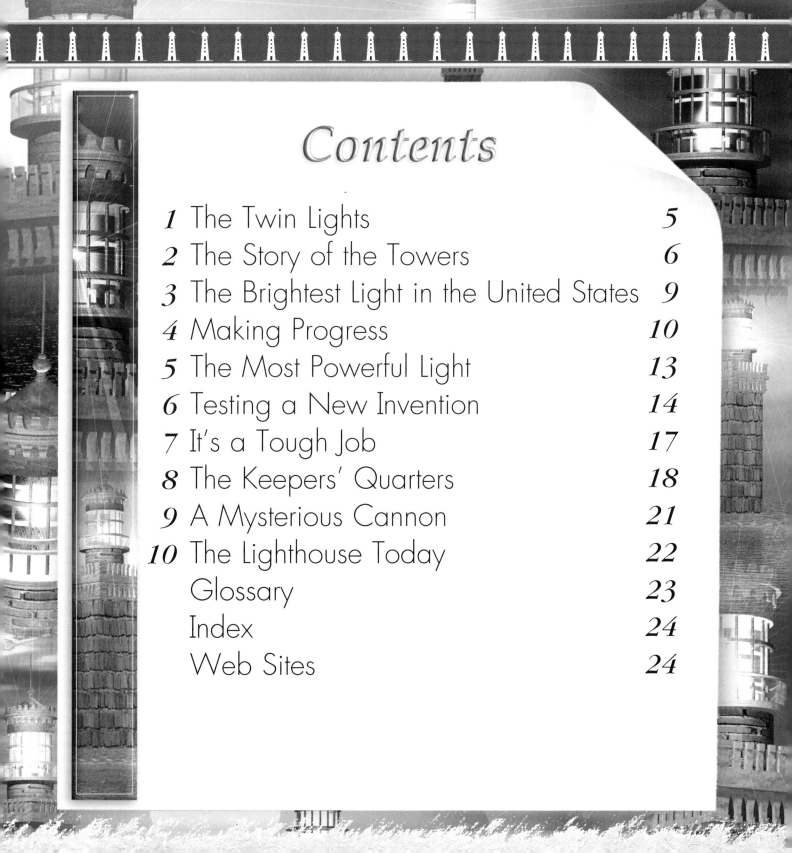

Contents

The Navesink Twin Lights once had the most powerful beam of any U.S. lighthouse. However, the lights at Navesink were put out in 1949.

The Twin Lights

The Navesink Twin Lights are located in Highlands, New Jersey. They were built on the highest point of the Atlantic coast's mainland. "Light" is another name for lighthouse. A lighthouse is a tower with a bright light at the top. This light helps to guide ships through rough seas. The first lighthouse was built in Egypt in 280 B.C. and was called Pharos. It is known as one of the seven wonders of the ancient world.

The Navesink lighthouse looks like a castle. Unlike many other lighthouses, it has two towers instead of one. The lights shone from a height of about 250 feet (76 m) above sea level. Many important firsts have taken place at this lighthouse, giving it a rich history.

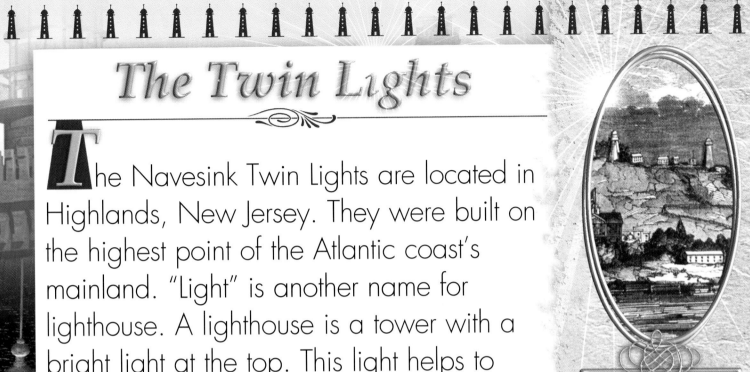

The Navesink Twin Lights built in 1828 were not attached to each other.

5

The Story of the Towers

In the mid-1700s, New York merchants built a lighthouse on the **highlands** of New Jersey. Its beam helped to guide boats into nearby New York Harbor. Little is known about this lighthouse. However in 1828, construction of the first Navesink Twin Lights was completed. The identical towers were made of blue split stone and stood 320 feet (97.5 m) from each other. They weren't connected. In time these lighthouses began to fall apart. The Navesink Twin Lights were rebuilt in 1862, with **brownstone**. This time the **architect**, Joseph Lederle, made the towers look different. The south tower was square, and the north one was **octagonal**. Lederle attached the towers with a long building.

Merchants are shown sailing toward the Navesink Twin Lights in this 1828 drawing.

6

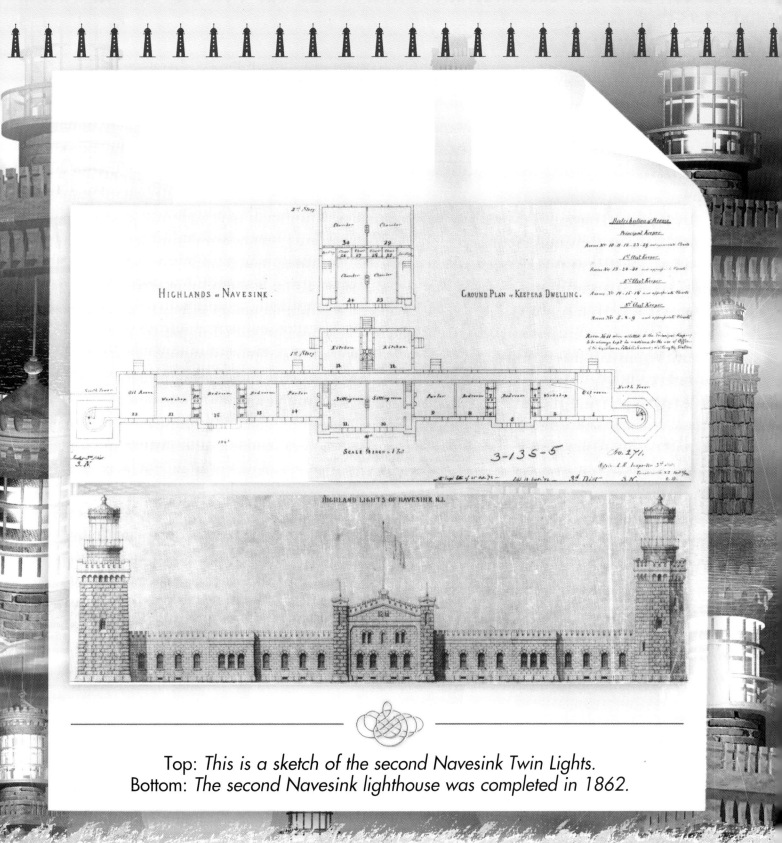

Top: *This is a sketch of the second Navesink Twin Lights.*
Bottom: *The second Navesink lighthouse was completed in 1862.*

LIGHTHOUSE LENS

No longer in use at the Navesink Twin Lights, this lens is on display there.

The Brightest Light in the United States

Navesink Twin Lights is famous for being the first lighthouse in the United States to use a Fresnel lens. This was a new type of lens that made the light easier to see from great distances. In 1838, Congress sent **Commodore** Matthew C. Perry to Europe to study lighthouses. He bought two Fresnel lenses in France and shipped them to New Jersey. One lens was used in each of Navesink's two towers. Augustin Fresnel invented the lens in 1822. It is shaped liked a glass beehive. The Fresnel lens uses glass **prisms** to **magnify** and to bend light into a powerful beam. In 1841, a steady light was placed in the south tower and a **revolving** light was placed in the north tower. Navesink then became brighter than any other U.S. lighthouse.

9

Making Progress

Some say the two Navesink towers look like chess pieces known as the king and queen.

The Fresnel lens comes in six different sizes called **orders**. A first order lens is the brightest. The south tower of the Navesink Twin Lights had a first order lens, and the north tower had a second order lens. Even with these new lenses, it was often hard for ships to see the light on foggy nights. Lighthouse foghorns sent out loud signals to warn boats that the land was near. The first foghorns, used in the 1700s, were cannons. Fog bells and steam-driven whistles were used later. Before the invention of electricity, it took a lot of work to keep the lighthouse running. The light was lit with oil, and lighthouse keepers had to wind **gears** every few hours so the light would turn.

Visitors can climb to the top of the north tower of Navesink Twin Lights and enjoy a magnificent view of the ocean.

Top: *This is a 1939 photo of Navesink lighthouse keeper Murphy Rockette.*
Bottom: *In 1898, this electric powerhouse was built at the Navesink Twin Lights.*

The Most Powerful Light

Navesink was the first **primary** lighthouse in the United States to make its own electricity. In 1898, a building was set up at Navesink for this purpose. A new, electric arc lamp replaced the south tower's beehive light. This new light had a **candlepower** of 25 million. One candlepower is the amount of light coming from a single candle. The new light was so bright that some ships claimed they could see it from more than 70 miles (113 km) away. The light in the north tower was no longer needed. In 1917, it was necessary to change the electric lamp to an oil light to lower costs. The candlepower dropped to about 700,000. In the 1930s, electricity was restored. The candlepower became 9 million and stayed there until the light went out of service in 1949.

Testing a New Invention

In 1899, Guglielmo Marconi was invited to the United States from England to test his new invention. Marconi had invented the wireless **telegraph**. This machine can send messages to other places without the use of wires. Marconi set up the equipment at the Navesink Twin Lights. He was supposed to send and receive messages about a boat race, but the race was postponed. It was postponed because Commodore George Dewey had come back **victorious** from a battle in the Spanish-American War. This war between Spain and the United States began in 1898. It dealt in part with Cuba's fight for **independence** from Spain, which America supported. The telegraph was used for the first time in history, to report about the commodore and his **fleet**. The Navesink Twin Lights became the first station capable of sending and receiving messages regularly.

For many years, a telegraph station (left) stood next to Navesink Twin Lights.
This station provided communication to ships sailing to and from New York.

Items on display at the
Twin Lights Historic Site
museum include
lifesaving service tools
and clothing.

Recent funding
has allowed the
museum to
improve its
displays.

On display at the museum are equipment
and materials from ships and sailors.

It's a Tough Job

The Navesink Twin Lights had one principal lighthouse keeper and three assistant keepers to help keep it running. Lighthouse keepers had to trim the wick on the light and make sure there was enough oil. They had to wind the gears so the light would turn. They had to make sure the machinery was working properly. They worked very long hours in the cold, damp towers. The keepers were highly dedicated to their jobs. If they made a mistake, or if the light went out, that would mean danger for ships at sea. The keepers' jobs were sometimes dangerous, too. In 1883, a keeper named John Smith accidentally set himself on fire while lighting the south tower. Even though he had been burned, he made sure the light was working properly.

The Keepers' Quarters

Murphy Rockette was the last principal lighthouse keeper at the Navesink Twin Lights. He retired in 1952.

Most lighthouse keepers were former sea captains or sailors. Through the years, there were more than 12 principal keepers and more than 70 assistants at the Navesink Twin Lights. The main Keepers' Quarters were in the long building between the two towers. The principal keeper had four or five rooms. The assistants lived in the lower sections at either end of the building. The keepers often lived at the lighthouse with their families. Before the 1920s, there was no indoor plumbing, heating, or electricity in the Keepers' Quarters. Keepers tended this lighthouse until 1949. That year the U.S. **Coast Guard** decided to put out the lights of Navesink.

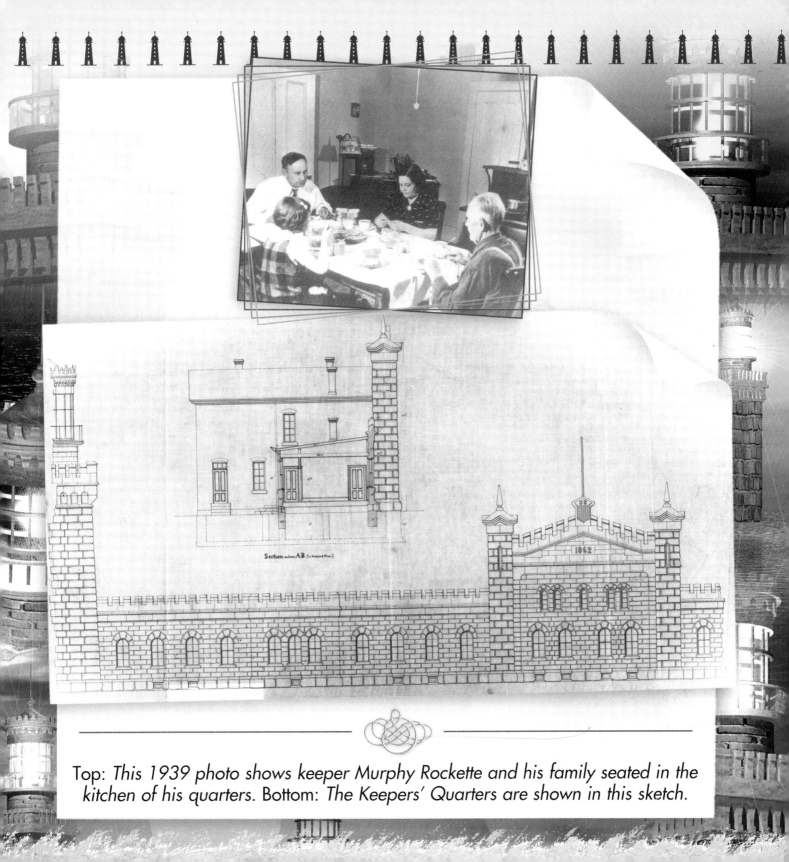

Top: *This 1939 photo shows keeper Murphy Rockette and his family seated in the kitchen of his quarters.* Bottom: *The Keepers' Quarters are shown in this sketch.*

The design of Navesink Twin Lights reminds some onlookers of an ancient castle.

A Mysterious Cannon

In 1841, a cannon was found buried on the grounds. No one knew how the cannon got there. Some thought it was a pirate's cannon. Others thought it was used during the American Revolution. It also could have been fired as a fog signal during foggy weather, to warn ships of danger. There is one clue, however. The markings on it read "1756 xx J * Lopez." Lopez was a keeper at the lighthouse when the cannon was first dug up. No one is sure why he **engraved** the date 1756 into the cannon. Some believe that 1756 was the year the first lighthouse was built on this site. No one can be sure where the cannon came from, but it is still kept on the lighthouse grounds today.

The Lighthouse Today

In 1949, after 121 years of service, the lights at Navesink were put out. This was because new **navigational** aids, such as **radar**, came into use. Lighthouses are no longer needed as in the past, but some still operate. They are **automated**. This means they run on their own and don't need keepers to make the lights shine. In 1960, a small light was turned on in the north tower of Navesink as a reminder of days gone by. That same year, the lighthouse opened as a historical site. Visitors to the lighthouse can climb the north tower all the way to the top. At the top, one gets a sense of the Twin Lights' place in U.S. history.

Navesink is known as a lighthouse of many firsts.

Glossary

architect (AR-kih-tekt) Someone who designs buildings.

automated (AW-tuh-mayt-ed) When something operates on its own without help.

brownstone (BROWN-stohn) A reddish brown sandstone used for building.

candlepower (KAN-duhl-pow-uhr) The amount of light coming from one candle.

coast guard (KOHST GARD) The part of the military that controls the waters.

commodore (KAH-muh-dor) An officer in the navy in charge of a group of ships.

engraved (en-GRAYVD) To have carved into a hard surface such as metal.

fleet (FLEET) Many ships under the command of one person.

gears (GEERZ) 1. Wheels with teeth on the edge. 2. Parts of a machine that help it to work.

highlands (HY-luhndz) A high or hilly part of a country.

independence (in-dih-PEN-dents) Freedom from the control or help of other people.

magnify (MAG-nih-fy) To make light appear stronger than it is.

navigational (nah-vuh-GAY-shuh-nuhl) Having to do with the science of figuring out the position and course of ships.

octagonal (ok-TA-guh-nul) Having eight sides.

orders (OR-derz) The sizes of the Fresnel lens that determine the brightness and distance the light will travel.

primary (PRY-mair-ee) Main; greatest in importance.

prisms (PRIH-zuhmz) Solid objects made of glass used to bend light.

radar (RAY-dar) A system that uses sound waves to locate objects.

revolving (rih-VOLV-ing) Turning.

telegraph (TEH-luh-graf) A machine that uses signals to communicate.

victorious (vik-TOR-ee-uhs) Having won something, such as a battle or a race.

Index

Web Sites

To learn more about the Navesink Twin Lights, check out these Web sites:

http://members.aol.com/houselite/navesink.htm
http://njlhs.burlco.org/twinlights.htm

24